LITTLE STORIES of a BIG GOD

To the Bethel Family~
"Oh, how He loves you & me!"
Hope Harrington Kolb

LITTLE STORIES of a BIG GOD

Hope Harrington Kolb

Hope House
P.O. Box 428377
Chicago, IL 60642

LITTLE STORIES of a BIG GOD

Hope House
P.O. Box 428377
Chicago, IL 60642

*Copyright © 1992
by Hope Harrington Kolb
All Rights Reserved*

Library of Congress Catalog Card Number: 92-85266

ISBN: 0-9635250-2-6

Printed in the United States of America

*Dedicated
with love,
appreciation,
and
precious memories,*

*to
Daddy,*

Rev. George R. Harrington,

*who was always
saying to his children,*

*"Let me read
you
something
good."*

My Dear Reader....

The following Little Stories are true, taken from my own and my family's experiences.

Some are dramatic, and some are about God's "everyday" care for people who love and obey Him...a marvel in itself!

If you know the Big God they are about, then no doubt you have many such stories in your own life to share with others, and I hope this book will inspire you to do just that.

If you don't know Him, my heart's prayer is that these Little Stories will cause you to yearn for and accept as your Savior and Lord, Jesus Christ, Who is the all-powerful Big God, but Who is also the dearest, closest "everyday" Friend a human being can ever have.

Hope

THE LITTLE STORIES

1..................Subway Satyr
2..................At 11:45 P.M.
3........Operation Prayer Room
4..................Daddy's Vision
5................Cocoa's Puppies
6........The Middle of Nowhere
7..........Little "Yellow Eyes"
8.............Decision at 3 A.M.
9.............Babe In the Woods
10....Old Sister Luker's Angel
11.........."Dog's Best Friend"
12.........The Cursing Blessing
13...........Balcony Visitation
14...................Broken Baby
15........Stranger In the Night
16...................The Robbery
17............My Sister's Hands
18.................Two Sparrows
19.................Washer Wonder
20.................Drunk Attack!
21.............Strange Exchange
22..................Double's Day
23....................Little One
24................One Last Move

Subway Satyr

I knew his face well:
Long and thin, framed by
Sharply pointed ears...
Just like a satyr.
He was always on my train,
Always watching,
Staring at me with
Those huge, dark eyes.

He never spoke to me.
Never followed me.
So I tried to ignore him.
If I'd been suspicious
Of every strange-looking
Character on the subway,
I'd have become paranoid.

But one night was different:
The satyr got off the train
At my stop...something he'd
Never done before.

Someone behind me spoke.
I knew it was the satyr
Even before I turned
And saw him staring at me,
Just a few feet away...

My heart was in my throat.
But he spoke politely:
"Miss, you have something
Stuck on your shoe."

His eyes went to my feet,
And I looked down just
For the barest instant.

In a flash he was there,
Grabbing my ankle and leg,
Forcing me against the wall.
My mind skidded toward terror,
But I struggled and broke away,
Running pellmell down the
Stairs toward the street,
His steps sounding behind me.

I remembered all the
Dark alleys and dirty bars
On my way home...
Could I hope to outrun him?

And then I saw it:
A carload of Chicago cops
Sitting right there in
Front of me....just
Waiting to rescue me.

They saw me home
Safe & sound.

Some of my generation
Called them "pigs".

I thought they were angels.

At 11:45 P.M.

*We were in love,
So it was hard
To part and go
Our separate ways...
He to the East,
I further West.*

*A Texas highway
Can be a lonely place
Late at night,
With only the stars
And cattle
And mesquite trees
For company.*

*But I didn't
Feel alone,
Having the Lord
To talk to...
I was completely
At peace,
When out of the blue
I had a sudden,
Heart-shaking feeling
That something
Was wrong.
I had to pray--
Right away!--
For him.*

*I pulled off
At a tiny town
And found a spot
Under a streetlamp
And prayed there,
Earnestly! Urgently!
Not knowing why.
I looked at my watch:
It was 11:45 p.m.*

*Later, I called him.
"Did you have a good trip?"
I asked.*

*He was silent for a moment.
"I wasn't going to tell you,"
He said, "but tonight
I fell asleep at the wheel
And came within an inch
Of hitting a concrete wall
At sixty miles an hour,*

At 11:45 p.m."

Operation Prayer Room

*The pain was excruciating.
I went to my classes
But sat at the back
Where I could bend over
And grasp my ankles to
Alleviate some of the
Agony....*

*It was kidney disease,
And the doctors had tried
Everything: old drugs,
New drugs, and specialists.
Nothing helped. I grew worse.
And my doctor was deeply
Concerned.*

*One day, I went into the
Little private prayer room
In my dorm, to pray...
I'd prayed often before,
But nothing had happened.*

This time something did.

*I prayed quietly, but
In earnest. I was in
Desperate need.
And as I prayed, I felt
A warm something -- only
The Lord knows what --
In that part of my back
Which housed the pain.*

*It was almost like a
Surgeon's knife...but
Wielded gently, with
An anesthetic applied.*

*The next day I saw the
Doctor...Would my tests
Tell me I had imagined
My prayer-room operation?*

*I held my breath: but no,
For the first time in
More than a year,
The lab reports were
NEGATIVE.*

*I told my doctor what had
Happened the day before.
He was a Christian &
Not altogether skeptical.
Still, he warned:
"Don't be surprised if
This comes back at some
Point in your life. It
Often does, you know."*

Oh, ye of little faith!

*He's gone now, but I
Wish he could know:
That prayer-room operation
Was a total success...*

More than twenty years ago.

Daddy's Vision

*He was not a young man,
Though I was only nine
When it happened.*

*We lived in a duplex because
The church had no building,
So the church worshipped
In one side of our house.
Or we lived in one side
Of the church--
Whichever way you saw it.*

*We kids had it made:
Kittens, and Bible school,
And bikes.
But Daddy was tired...
Painting houses all day long
And pastoring, too...
Visiting and counseling and
Preaching every week.*

*He went to bed exhausted--
One night so bone-weary
He wondered how long
He could go on this way.
He slept--how could he
Keep from it?*

*But at three o'clock
In the morning,
Something happened.
A never-before and
Never-since Something.*

*Something so special
That he has told
Few people about it
In the years between.*

*He says he was awakened
From his sleep
By a feeling that someone
Had come into the room.
He looked: and there,
Seated in a chair
Beside his bed,
Was the Lord Jesus...
Just looking at Daddy
With the kindest,
Most encouraging
Look.*

*Daddy says he knew
It was a vision,
But the Lord was really there,
Like a real person--
Not ghostlike at all.
Real enough to reach out
And touch.
And just sitting there
Looking at him
With such compassion
And reassurance.
And then He was gone.*

*Daddy says
He was a new man
The next morning.*

No wonder.

Cocoa's Puppies

*I remember so many things
About the place where we
Lived when I was twelve.*

*The old tire swing,
The pond with goldfish
The size of trout...
Skating on the sidewalks,
Dressing up in playclothes
And singing, "Frankie and
Johnny were sweethearts"...*

*But I remember
Cocoa's puppies best,
And the night
It rained so hard.
Our house was small,
So Cocoa and her puppies
Were outside under the house
In a cardboard box...
Sweet little bundles of love,
So soft and helpless,
Their eyes still closed,
With that special smell
Only tiny puppies have.
How I loved them!*

*No one worried about the rain.
This was West Texas, and
We didn't have many floods.
It was Mother who remembered
Cocoa and her puppies
And decided to check on them.*

*When she opened the door,
There was the water knee-high!
And Cocoa's puppies floating
On the water in their
Soggy cardboard box about
To break through the bottom.*

*I would have died
A thousand deaths to find
Our precious pets drowned...
But it was Mother who rescued
Cocoa and her puppies.*

*Strange...Mother wasn't
Dog-crazy and could have
Lived without them.
But it seems to me
When I remember that night...
Perhaps she really loved them
More than any of us did.*

The Middle of Nowhere

*I've heard people say
That the Lord takes care
Of fools and children,
And right then I felt
Like a little bit of both.*

*Young and single, driving alone
Across the Arizona desert
In the middle of a blazing
Mid-August day,
The temperature well over
A hundred degrees,
With a gas tank
Sitting on Empty,
And nothing in sight
Except sand and more sand
Stretching all the way
To California.*

*Then I saw it.
A tiny dirt road
Leading even further
Into the middle of Nowhere,
But my only hope
Of finding gasoline
In time.*

*And at the end of it,
A ghost-station
Complete with caved-in tin roof
And broken windows,
Tumbleweeds up to the eaves
And rusty gas pumps
Abandoned for many a year.*

*But no--a lazy hound dog stirred,
And inside the decrepit building,
An old man, prospector-type,
Was serving sandwiches.
And there was gas.
Thank the Lord!*

*"Where you from?" he drawled,
Almost too much a part
Of the past to be a real
Part of the present.
"Anderson, Indiana," I told him.
"That so?" he said nonchalantly.
"Fellow came through here
A few months ago from there,
Bikin' all the way to Californy."
He named the young man.
"Ever hear of him?"*

*Incredibly, I had.
I told the old man how
The boy had been almost
Killed in a terrible accident,
But the church had prayed,
And God had spared his life.
And we talked a while longer,
That old-time prospector and I,
Out there in the middle
Of Somewhere.*

Little "Yellow Eyes"

*Out near the dusty little town
Of Gorman, Texas, stands an
Old church campground --
Silent now, but a reminder
Of pleasant days & past joys.
I stood there not long ago
And pictured it back then...*

*She was just four years old,
A lively little girl
With big, hazel eyes,
Running and playing at an
Old-fashioned campmeeting
Out on the sunny plains...
When suddenly one day her
Hazel eyes were no longer hazel
But yellow as a ripe banana,
And so was her skin.*

*The lively little girl
Stopped running and playing,
And she stopped eating
And drinking, too.*

*"Yellow jaundice," the adults
Said, shaking their heads sadly.
"Will you pray for her?"
Her father asked the ministers,
His heart heavy.*

*They prayed, but nothing
Happened.
And the little girl
Grew worse.*

*"We'll just have to muster up
Faith ourselves," her Daddy
Said to her Mother.
And they did.*

*The next day the little girl
With the big, hazel eyes
Was running and playing again.*

*I smiled as I pictured that
Little girl today...
A busy pastor's wife with a
Lively little girl of her own.*

*What a difference a Daddy &
Mother with faith can make
In the life of a little girl!*

Decision At 3 A.M.

*The Capitol glowed in the
Spring moonlight....
Washington was lovely
This time of year.
But I was distressed.
Something had happened
To make me wonder if
Something were interfering
With God's hearing
And answering my prayers.*

*I prayed for a sign:
To have my husband
Cancel our plan to attend
A certain Civil War
Re-enactment
The following day...
And to do it
Before morning.*

*What a miracle that
Would be!
We had come all this way
For that very purpose!
And there were few things
He enjoyed more.*

*I waited all day,
But he said nothing...
Nothing, that is, except
How eager he was for
Tomorrow.*

*We went to bed.
Still, silence and
No change of heart.
I was careful not to
Say anything that might
Influence him.
I truly wanted an
Answer from God.
I lay down feeling sad and
Discouraged, thinking,
"I guess I have my answer."*

*At 3 a.m. he woke me.
"I don't know why
I'm feeling this way,"
He said, puzzled.
"But I don't think
We should go to the
Re-enactment today.
Would you be disappointed
If we did something else?"*

*I almost cried with relief
And told him how I'd prayed.
"It's funny," he said,
"But I struggled with whether
Or not to wake you up and
Tell you now. I hated to
Wake you in the
Middle of the night, but
I had this strange urge
To tell you that I'd
Decided not to go, and
To tell you before morning."*

Strange....but wonderful.

Babe In the Woods

*It was late at night,
And the Louisiana Woods
Were deep and dark
With a darkness only
Those who've been there
Can imagine.*

*I wasn't born yet,
But I can see them...
Mother watching anxiously
For the tiny, one-lane road
That would lead them to
Aunt Josie's house...
Daddy driving competently,
Untroubled by the darkness...
My sisters in the backseat,
Two and four years old,
Rubbing their eyes sleepily,
Beyond the point of asking,
"Are we there yet?"*

*Then, suddenly, Daddy
Stopped the car
Dead in its tracks:
There before them lay
Not one tiny road,
But five tiny roads!
All equally dark...
All equally unmarked...
All equally unfamiliar.*

How could they know
Which way to go?
Which one to take?
And it was so late!
And so dark!
In the Louisiana Woods.

Then, from the backseat
A little voice began to sing,
"I know the Lord will make
A way for me....
If I live a holy life,
Shun the wrong and
Do the right,
I know the Lord will
Make a way for me!"

Daddy smiled and
Chose a road.
It was, of course,
The one which led
Straight to
Aunt Josie's house.

Old Sister Luker's Angel

*One of my mother's memoirs
Makes me wish I could have
Known old Sister Luker.
She must have been special,
This sweet, elderly saint
In a church my parents
Pastored before I was born.*

*Sister Luker had cancer,
And the doctors told her
She would die any day now...
But her dear granddaughter
Was expecting a baby,
And that baby would be
Old Sister Luker's
Very first great-grandchild.*

*Could the Lord please
Let her live long enough
To see it? she prayed.
He could, He did,
And old Sister Luker
Lived to see her
Precious progeny.*

*Very soon afterward,
A neighbor reported
Strange happenings over
At old Sister Luker's house.*

"An angel came,"
The neighbor said,
"To Sister Luker's
Bedroom window
And hovered a while...
Then the angel went
Around to the front door
And entered."

"Nonsense!" someone scoffed.
Someone else asked,
"What time was that?"
The neighbor named the hour
She had seen the angel
Enter the house.

"How strange!" they all agreed,
And then they told her:
That had been the very hour
Of old Sister Luker's death.

"Dog's Best Friend"

*His name was Duke,
And he was dying.*

*He lay listlessly,
This sweet Cocker Spaniel,
About to leave a world
Where he was dearly loved
And would be sadly missed.*

*Duke was dying,
And my sister's heart
Was breaking.*

*She was just a little girl,
But she had a big heart,
And she ached for this
Helpless, hurting creature,
Even though he belonged to
Someone else.*

*She prayed for him,
Faith-full child
That she was;
And the Lord touched him,
Faithful God that He is.*

*The very next day
Duke was no longer dying,
But running & playing
With my sister.*

*Some might scoff at that,
Thinking an animal unworthy
Of God's attention.*

*But they have never read
About Balaam, where
The angel would have
Killed the man
But spared the donkey!*

*"A righteous man has regard
For the life of his beast."
That's Bible authority.*

*Now, dogs are called
"Man's Best Friend"...
But anyone who knows God
Knows that <u>He</u> is
"Man's Best Friend".*

*Maybe they just don't
Realize He's
"Dog's Best Friend", too.*

The Cursing Blessing

*Daddy was an evangelist
Across the South
In the 1950's....
We traveled as a family,
And the memories
We made together!*

*We girls sang specials,
And Mother led the singing,
And while it was wonderful,
Sometimes there
Wasn't much money.
Once, we had to stop traveling
When one of our tires blew out
And there was no cash to
Buy another one.*

*Then one day a man
Backed into us
And smashed a window.
He cursed and cursed
Until Mother asked
Him to stop.
He paid for the window,
But instead of fixing it,
We taped it up and bought
The tire we needed
To go on to the next church!*

*Maybe a few people looked at us
And felt sorry for us kids,
Having to move around so much.
But I wouldn't have traded places
With a princess in a palace!*

*That man's cursing
Was the only time
In my childhood
I ever heard anything besides
Kind words and loving voices,
Laughter and gentle conversation...
The only time in my childhood
I ever heard a voice raised
In anger or cursing.*

*And even that was turned
Into a blessing!*

Balcony Visitation

*The Lord is very real
To me, so I am never
Surprised by a sense
Of His presence...
But on one occasion
He was so real
I'm not sure I can
Explain it.*

*I was in an old
Victorian Hotel,
Close to Christmas,
And while I should
Have been joyful,
I was deeply troubled.*

*The cause is
Irrelevant...but
My lack of peace
Was painful, and
I wandered out onto
My sixth-floor
Balcony for a
Look at the mighty
Mississippi
Shining in the
Southern sunshine,
Not so far away.*

*Now, I have felt the
Presence of Jesus
Many times...so real
And sweet it has
Moved me to tears.*

*But this time...it was
A Little Different.*

*I was leaning on the
Balcony railing,
Not really praying,
Just feeling troubled...
When I knew
I wasn't alone.*

*It didn't last long.
In fact, it was so gentle
It was almost imperceptible,
But as real as my hands &
Feet...and as close.
Like a gentle,
Refreshing breeze,
He was there,
Moving so near me
And so distinctly
That I had to lean back
To let Him pass...
And He said to me --
So clearly I can feel
The comfort to this day! --
"Rest in me. I love you."*

*I can't explain it.
I only know it turned
My heart around. And I
Was at rest in His love
In a very special way
As a result of that
Balcony Visitation.*

Broken Baby

*I've always felt
Deeply thankful for
My growing-up years
Spent with faithful
Christian parents....
But never more than when
Mother tells me the story
Of what happened when
I was about one year old.*

*She was lying on the bed
Playing with me,
Holding me high above her,
Tossing me in the air
A little, as grownups
Often do with babies...
When down I came
In just the wrong way--
And my neck was broken.*

*Mother was terrified.
Shaking, she called an older
Saint in their congregation,
Who came and prayed for me.*

*She says I returned to
Normalcy immediately
And went right to sleep--
Sleeping so soundly
That her faith wavered
And she thought
I was dead!*

*Obviously, I wasn't;
And I've often thought
How different my life
Would have been
Were it not for
Christian parents
Who believed in God's power...*

*...Over almost before
It had begun!*

*In a way, that accident
Was a blessing.
I think knowing that
God spared me as a baby
Has made me determined
Not to make Him wish He
Had let me come to Him
At that early,
Innocent age...*

*...And determined to
Please Him with
The life He returned to me
So many years ago.*

Stranger In the Night

*It was a chilly night,
And dense fog swirled
About me as I drove along
The California coast,
Just feet away from the
Ocean waves I could hear
Crashing against the
Rocky coast below...*

*At first the little
White lines led me,
And then I was
Driving blind,
In danger of plunging
Onto sharp rocks
A hundred feet down.*

*"Oh, Lord," I breathed,
"Please help me!"
How many times
Had I said those words?
And the Lord had never
Ignored my cry.*

*Almost immediately,
A light pierced the fog,
And there was a place to
Pull off the road to safety.
I stumbled through the fog
And knocked on the door
Of the first house I saw.*

A young woman welcomed me:
Did I need a place to stay?
Police were closing
All the roads in the area.

That night I slept on a
Stranger's couch in San Diego.
"Risky!" friends exclaimed.
But I knew it hadn't been.
We'd talked about the Lord
Until the wee hours
And hugged each other
Like sisters when I left
The next morning.

It was the worst fog
San Diego had seen in years,
And 8 people died that night
On the roads and highways...
I could have been
One of them so easily.

I left my hostess a gift
Inscribed: "To a 'stranger
In the night' who never was
Really a stranger at all...

Because our visit was
Arranged by a Friend."

The Robbery

*They were sleeping in their car
And eating out of cans
Stored in the backseat.
They were destitute,
So we invited them
To our home.*

*We gave them a spare room
And a televison set
And found the young man a job.
We ate and did dishes together,
Talked and laughed,
And for the next ten days,
They lived with us.*

*Then one day on my way home
I had a feeling that I
Shouldn't go home just then.
It was a strange feeling,
And quite strong.
So I stopped and bought a
Coke and a newspaper and
Arrived home an hour
Later than usual.*

*My husband rushed out
With tears in his eyes
And threw his arms around me.
"I was so worried!" he said.
"They're gone. They stole
Our television set, radios,
Tape decks, money and checks,*

*And worst of all, my shotgun.
I was so afraid you had
Walked in on them and they
Had taken you with them
Or hurt you."*

*We called the police.
"You're lucky to be alive!"
They told us. "That man is
A convicted felon. What
Time did the robbery happen?"*

*We said we weren't sure, but
I remembered the strong feeling
That had kept me away from home
And thought perhaps I knew.*

*Friends told us we were crazy
For taking in strangers
Off the street. Maybe.
But the One Who told us to be
Hospitable to strangers--
That we might entertain angels--
Protected us...*

*And we never even missed
What these all-too-human
Guests stole that day.
He has replaced it all
So many times over!*

My Sister's Hands

I've watched her use her hands
To prepare thousands of meals
For ministers and missionaries
From all over the world,
For her extended family,
And for strangers...
A dozen dishes
That melt in your mouth,
And the best Southern tea
This side of Heaven.

And I've watched her play
Thousands of songs on the piano
For as many worship services,
And write thousands of Get Well,
Birthday, and Anniversary cards
For just about everyone in the
World--and always a little
Personal note at the bottom
Of every card.

And then I think of that day
Long ago, when a young mother
Accidentally slammed the
Car door shut on her
Little girl's hand.

She screamed, and so did
My sister, who was only
Five years old at the time,
And whose hand was so small
And so terribly crushed.

*Then a sweet Christian lady
Took that tiny hand in hers
Like a soft, broken bird
And asked the Lord Jesus
To touch it and make it well.
No melodrama...
No shouting to Heaven...
No demands...just a quiet
Prayer in simple faith,
Asking a Friend for help.*

*My sister's hands are perfect...
Simply beautiful.
And so has her service been to
That Friend ever since that day.*

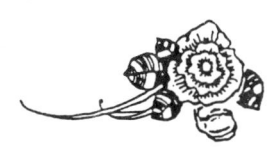

Two Sparrows

*It was a sight I'd always
Dreaded: that of a
Little bird--a sparrow--
Attacked by the family dog.
Torn and bleeding, it
Flopped around in agony
While I watched
In helpless horror.*

*My heart hammered as I
Dragged the dog back
Inside the house, praying
That God would help the
Poor bird...it would never
Survive, I knew. Its wings
Had been almost torn off.
I ached at the thought
Of having to put it
Out of its misery.
Could I even do it?*

*I prayed desperately:
"Please, Lord...I know I'm
Asking a lot...it's just a
Little bird...but please, Lord,
Help the poor thing...
Please, please, please!"*

*I went back outside and
Resolutely started toward
Where the little sparrow
Had been suffering,
Dreading the awful sight...*

He was no longer there!

*Frantically I searched the
Whole area in surprise
And consternation,
Not daring to believe the
Answer to my own prayer.*

There was no one around.

*No people...no animals....
The silence was profound.*

*And I had been gone
Less than a minute.*

*I don't suppose I'll ever
Know what happened...*

*But I have a feeling
The One Who told
His disciples that not even
The smallest sparrow
Falls to the ground apart
From the Heavenly Father...*

*...Was watching out for
Two sparrows that day.*

Washer Wonder

*Daddy's first priority
Has always been
The Lord's work, but he
Worked at a regular
Job, too, since he had a
Special burden for small
Churches who couldn't
Always afford a
Fulltime pastor...*

*One day he was working
On the roof of a house,
Which wasn't unusual
For him...But this time,
He was wearing slick shoes,
And he slipped and plunged--
Not to the ground, which
Would have been bad enough,
But right onto an
Old-fashioned washer--
The kind with
A steel wringer
Jutting out on top!*

*It could have injured
Him for life.
It should have broken
Something, at least.*

*But he got up and walked
Away as if nothing at all
Had happened.*

*His eyeglasses had flown off
And landed on the ground
Several feet away...*

*But even they were
Unbroken.*

*What is it the Scripture
Says? "For He will give
His angels charge
Concerning you...
They will bear you up
In their hands,
Lest you strike your foot
Against a stone."*

*And even when you strike
Something harder than
A stone...*

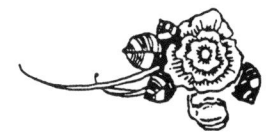

20

Drunk Attack!

*God's love can lead into
Strange situations,
And this is one of them...
Alone on the subway
In one of Chicago's most
Notorious ghettos...
Alone, that is, except for
The black student beside me
And the black drunk
Behind us -- dishevelled,
Reeking of whiskey and
Body odor, fingernails
Like an animal's claws,
Yellow eyes bulging,
Full of venom as he
Drunkenly glares at us,
Mumbling, "Black and white
Shouldn't sit together."*

*He means it: his filthy
Fingers reach out for the
Backs of our necks
And we scream in horror,
Jumping to run--
But there is nowhere to run!
Can we leave the train
And take the chance
He'll follow us?
No. We must wait...
And we must leave <u>together</u>
Or face even more danger.*

*But the chances of leaving
This train at the same stop,
With dozens of stops
Along this route--?
Almost nil. I ask anyway:
"Which is your stop?",
Dreading the answer.
She names it and I stare:
It is my stop, too!*

*Amazing coincidence!
What was it the drunk
Had mumbled?
I couldn't recall
At the moment
But thought perhaps
God had had
Another Opinion.*

Strange Exchange

*Daddy often said it was
As if a magic wand had
Been waved over our lives.
But of course we knew it
Wasn't magic...it was
The Lord's blessings.*

*The Lord was our doctor,
Our insurance agent, and
Our mechanic more than once.*

*He was even our grocer
On occasion.
I remember Mother's story
About one time in particular.*

*We needed cash for food,
So Daddy was out selling
Bible Storybooks.*

*He came to a house where the
Lady had seven small children.*

*How they clamored for
That Bible Storybook!
But the woman had no cash
To pay for it.*

*Daddy would have given
It to her free of charge,
But she said, "No, wait."*

*Then she went out back
And returned with a
Big, red rooster!*

*I've often wondered what ever
Became of those seven children.
I know what happened to
The rooster! The cash from one
Bible Storybook wouldn't have
Fed our whole family,
But that rooster became
Our Christmas Dinner
Right in the middle of July!*

*It was a Strange Exchange,
I suppose, at least for America.
But Daddy needed physical food
For his children, and the woman
Needed spiritual food for hers,
So what could have been better?*

*Not a magic wand...just one of
Those minor "everyday miracles"
That the libraries of the world
Couldn't contain if they were
All written down in
Little Stories like these.*

22

Double's Day

He was so glad to see me...
Big, brown eyes glowing
With affection...
But rising to greet me,
Screams of anguish!
Hind legs buckling!
Some unexplained malady
Striking this sweet-faced dog
I love so much.

Collapsed body and
Cries of pain
Made my heart race.
How could I help him?
He wouldn't let me touch him!
Howls of agony
From an invisible trap
I couldn't see or loosen...
How could I bear it
Another moment?

Aloud I prayed
In desperation:
"Oh, Jesus, please
Help us!"

The next moment,
The shaking stopped.
The agonized cries
Subsided into silence,
And Double let me
Hold him.

*We sat on the floor
Together this way
For a little while...
He, exhausted by his sudden
Battle with unexpected terror,
And I, so relieved
I could have cried.*

*Finally, he lifted his eyes
To mine as if to say,
"Thank you."*

*And that is what I said
To the Lord:
"Thank you, Lord,
For all the times you've
Come to my rescue!"*

Little One

She was frightened and
Discouraged...and sick.

She was a classic candidate
For an abortion....
Past forty, with a lingering
Case of severe hepatitis,
And other physical problems.

The doctors warned that
She should at least undergo
Amniocentesis, which would
Tell her if the fetus
(Which my sister fortunately
Understood simply means
"Little One") might be
Deformed or handicapped.

"No," she replied. "I wouldn't
Kill this baby, whatever you
Might find. We are trusting
God to take care of it."

I recall watching her as
The baby grew within her...
There were times when her
Sweet, usually cheerful face
Carried a sad, worried look.
She surely wouldn't have been
Human if she hadn't
Wondered at times how
It would all turn out.

*Finally the long wait ended,
And the Day of Reckoning
Arrived.*

*The baby who was supposed
To be such a serious problem
Was born just two short hours
After the first warning.
I think about that every time
She comes flying to hug me
And make me glad she's alive...
This precious "little one"
The doctors were so
Willing to kill.*

*Her bedroom shelves are
Lined with athletic trophies,
Her report cards covered
With A's....She sings,
Plays the piano & the flute,
And she writes stories...*

*But none will ever match
Her own...the story of a
"Little one" who might have
Become an ugly statistic...*

*And instead became a
Beautiful Life.*

24

One Last Move

*She started out in a land
Of flowers & flamingos,
Palm trees swaying in
The balmy breeze...
Silver springs and
Deep blue ocean waters...
A tropical paradise.*

*But she gladly left
That place long ago for
"Anyplace, America"--
Anyplace God led her to
Serve with her husband....
They were a Team,
Mother and Daddy,
With a concern for
Little churches all
Across the country
In need of special help...*

*A city of millions,
A community of hundreds,
Big and little towns
And country in-between...
Even an island on a river.*

*So many moves!
So many houses!
So much work to be done
To make each house a home!
So many weary miles,
Boxes to pack and unpack...
So many changes to be made
With every move!*

*And then--One Last Move,
Far from that early
Tropical paradise.*

*Finally she rests --
Though only her memory
And her name --
Upon a dusty plain
Where sandstorms blow
And tumbleweeds get caught
Among the tombstones...
Where silent nights are
Broken by a hoot owl's cry
Atop the old mesquite
That stands beside
Her grave...*

*In life, her home was
Everywhere and Nowhere...
In death, she has a
Permanent Place.*

*And this time, I
Know Mother wouldn't
Change a thing.*

Photo by Scott Charles

About the Author......

Hope Harrington Kolb lives in a suburb of Chicago, but she grew up in parsonages across the Sunbelt, attending 14 public schools before college, in towns ranging from several hundred to several million people.

She is a minister, with a Bachelor of Arts degree in Music & Bible and a Master of Arts in Religion. And she is married to a minister, Rev. Jerry E. Kolb, who is also an executive for an international financial corporation headquartered in Chicago.

Hope has taught in the public schools of several states, at a church-related college in Alberta, Canada (Gardner Bible College, formerly Alberta Bible Institute), and at the University of Texas at Arlington while working toward a Ph.D. in Psychology.

She has traveled extensively throughout the U.S. and Canada as a speaker, concert artist and conference leader for conventions, churches, business and professional organizations, college convocations, public high school assemblies, civic groups, and other gatherings.

Her articles, poetry, and devotionals have appeared in publications by Warner Press (Anderson, Indiana) and in other periodicals.

To order copies of LITTLE STORIES OF A BIG GOD, mail this order form and a Check/Money Order for $5.00 per copy to:

Hope House
P.O. Box 428377
Chicago, IL 60642

Please add Shipping & Handling: $1.50 (1-5 copies); $2.00 (6-10 copies); $3.00 (11-20 copies). Please allow 3-4 weeks for delivery.

Number of Copies Ordered _____
x $5.00 each $ _____
Plus Shipping & Handling $ _____
TOTAL ENCLOSED $ _____

Name _____
Mailing Address _____
City _____ State ____ Zip ____
Phone _____